The Wealthy Expert: Where Finance Meets Success!"

Otto L. Eddings

Table of contents

Introduction

Chapter 1: Two keys of wealth

- Spend less
- Save more to invest

Chapter 2: The mindset leading to wealth

- The law of attraction
- Clutter

Chapter 3: How to scale with product

- Information
- Free vs cheap

Chapter 4: money vs time

- What is true wealth
- The large account

Conclusion

Introduction

Particularly the most significant thing to the greater part as we move on from training and begin in the realm of work is cash. It has turned into a critical piece of life!
What difference does this make it is important reason for everything that impact our lives
Cash is fundamental. However a couple of us knows how it functions, how to make it how to contribute it and how to have the right mentality to realize that how generally will be monetarily stable

Numerous new rich encounters and open doors opens up when you become well off not just that becoming affluent works on the outside things in one's day to day existence however it further develops an individual prosperity you become more sure you see life from a previously unheard-of point of view which permits you to articulate your thoughts and see life from another view completely. Which Empowers you to turn out to be more joyful than when you are battling monetarily.

The principal focal point of the book is dominating underpinnings of abundance I would say a many individuals neglect to accomplish abundance since they neglect to accomplish the essential structure blocks of money let center around it the majority of us neglect to put resources into our future since we don't have the assets accessible in any case Subsequently a crucial component of this book

is tied in with building an asset to have the
option to begin effective financial planning
My point is creation plan for your future in
abundance recollect that what makes is
genuinely rich is the time and capacity to would
what we like and when we need to and to
accomplish this we really want brilliant work
that what this is tied in with making and option
in contrast to your check

Chapter 1

Two keys of wealth

A large portion of us just need an essential comprehension of our funds. We needn't bother with a general capability like bookkeeping yet we have never been shown the premise. For my situation I was lucky in spite of the fact that my folks didn't show me planning.

The abundance creation issue is typically a result of how we carry on with our lives our bills begin to mount so we use Visa to facilitate the tight asset, we lease or purchase a house since we as a whole need some place to reside buy things for our homes go on vacations get a vehicle get hitched have children out of nowhere our compensations can deal with the costs intentions changed.

A requirement for monetary security replaces our great desire and dreams the additional obligation removes a greater amount of our extra energy to accompany our family and create extra income the outcomes can be destroying insights show that the high pace of separation is because of monetary difficulty on the off chance that you don't take this intensely serious now you might need to pay later.

Independence from the rat race is the point at which you get additional aloof unmerited pay from your resources and ventures than you pay out in everyday costs your recurring, automated revenue ought to keep on becoming no matter what your feedback.
Thus we should begin putting resources into wages procured resources as I referenced the most troublesome hindrances to this tis tracking down cash to contribute we should zero in on setting a cash to the side to accomplish this.

We should achieve two goals to set us in the best situation to begin creating financial momentum.

It doesn't occur onces it requires discipline and consistency until it turns into a way of life

What are the two keys to of building wealth

Spend less
Save more to invest

Let cover each to see if there is any improvement you can make to your current situation

Key 1:   spend less

We might think spending less is simple, however it is by no means simple. It is frequently difficult to eat less. The less you eat the more weight you lose the less you spend the more cash you need to put resources into your future.

The greater part of us never accomplish independence from the rat race since we spend our cash in our everyday living expense and excess is spent on things we want, but assuming we control our longings and spending then we could have begin to redirect a level of pay on something that appreciates and brings in our cash development.

The key is fostering the propensity for spending short of what you acquire as soon as could really be expected. Time and accruing funds wrap up. Indeed, even modest quantities saved reliably over many years develop dramatically. Short sprays of saving never create enduring financial stability.

Assuming that you're accustomed to spending all that you make, spending less requires addressing imbued propensities. Begin little - take a stab at preparing your lunch two times every week or skirting the day to day latte. Gather speed with little wins first.

The key is fostering the propensity for investing less Energy and accruing funds wrap up. Indeed, even modest quantities saved reliably over many years develop dramatically. Short sprays of saving never create enduring financial stability

Key 2: save more to invest

In this article, we will cover what saving is, what investing is, and the pros and cons of each, along with examples to help understand these concepts better.

KEY TAKEAWAYS

Setting aside cash implies putting away it securely so it is accessible when we really want it and it has a generally safe of losing esteem.

Venture accompanies risk, yet in addition the potential for better yields.Contributing normally frequently accompanies a more drawn out term skyline, for example, for youngsters' school assets or one's retirement. Both saving and contributing are key parts of one's individual budgets

What Is Saving?

 Saving is a phenomenal method for meeting momentary monetary objectives and plan for surprising circumstances, for example, a vehicle fix or doctor's visit expenses By setting to the side cash consistently,

 you can develop a pad that can assist you with enduring difficult stretches. Investment funds are for the most part okay, meaning your cash is protected, however the financing costs got are additionally low.

What Is Investing?

Contributing is a method for arriving at long haul monetary objectives, like putting something aside for school, an up front installment on a house, or retirement. Since financial planning implies facing some gamble, challenges' fundamental to pick ventures that line up with your objectives, risk resilience, and time skyline. By and large, the more you can contribute, the more gamble you can take on, in light of the fact that you have additional opportunity to brave the high points and low points of the stock marke Contributing is a method for arriving at long haul monetary objectives, like putting something aside for school, an up front installment on a house, or retirement. Since financial planning implies facing some gamble, challenges' fundamental to pick ventures that line up with your objectives, risk resilience, and time skyline. By and large, the more you can contribute, the more gamble you can take on, in light of the fact that you have additional opportunity to brave the high points and low points of the securities exchange.

Chapter 2
The mindset leading to wealth

It is vital and important to have the right and positive attitude prompting abundance

On the off chance that you dig further into the tales of well off individuals, you'll see a theme:

Seldom can a rich individual reduce their prosperity to a solitary wonderful second. All things being equal, they'll refer to their attitude as the most compelling motivation for their thriving.

An abundance outlook is a bunch of convictions, propensities, and ways of behaving that isolates the well off from the rest. An abundance mentality will direct you to capitalize on the cash you have.
Yet, it doesn't come simple. An abundance mentality implies spending less, making wise

ventures, and searching for ways of working on monetary remaining with negligible gamble. Fortunately with a touch of commitment, anybody can foster this mentality.

The law of attraction

Sooner or later in your life, you could have heard something about the examples of overcoming adversity of the rich and strong. Consistently, magazines and distributions, for example, Forbes run the rundown of the world's top very rich people. Jeff Bezos, Bill Entryways, Imprint Zuckerberg, Warren Buffett, and Elon Musk's names will quite often spring up close to noteworthy numbers.

As people, we follow these accounts with doubt in a specific level of profound respect, since, where it counts, we continually ponder the most ideal ways to secure riches. We endeavor to improve things, work on our status on the planet, and indeed, get more extravagant. Sooner or later in our lives, we are informed that the way to financial achievement is difficult work. "It's basic math", said creator T. Harv Eker "your pay can become exclusively to the degree that you do".

Appears to be truly straightforward, yet is it? Being rich is a propensity. However, the demonstrations and practices of adjustment follow an unmistakable brain process. The cycle is intricate and draws on a bunch of natural encounters, learned ways of behaving, and rehearses that advance the displaying of your current circumstance to stay recognizable, or re-making that commonality.

Some of the time, it involves others' discernments too. On the off chance that somebody acts in a way common of the very much behaved, individuals will respond to them as though they are well off. This just builds up that conviction and conduct in the luckily enriched, and a modern day miracle, they will carry a greater amount of that to themselves by distinguishing and supporting the way of behaving that "procures" it. What's more, those propensities, which to some extent have been learned in the well-to-do world they have a place with, will reproduce that world quite far. It additionally assists with supporting that custom by being in a climate that is homogenous and natural by seeing it around you and encountering it frequently.

Clutter

The propensities that outcome in a disordered living space can likewise prompt issues overseeing cash and keeping steady over funds. Confusion can influence your psychological wellness and influence how you bring in cash choices, from overspending and expanding obligation, to residing in greater and more costly homes.

Purchasing something once is a cost. In the event that it is something you really want and you use it, the cost is legitimate. On the off chance that you lose it and need to purchase another, that is a misuse of cash. In the event that you track down the primary thing yet it is demolished in light of the fact that it was under a heap of wet towels in the pantry, you'll need to purchase another while never profiting from the underlying consumption.

Chapter 3
How to scale with product

Plan how you want to increment deals. Then accept your orders multiplied or significantly increased for the time being. Does your association have individuals and frameworks to deal with those new orders, without falling flat or getting a major bruised eye? This is where a decent arrangement is fundamental.

The best preparation in my view begins with an itemized deals development gauge, separated by number of new clients, orders, and income you need to create. Incorporate a bookkeeping sheet that separates the numbers by month. The more unambiguous you are, the more practical your deals obtaining plan can be. Then, at that point, do a comparable cost conjecture, in view of adding innovation, individuals, framework, and frameworks to deal with that multitude of new deals orders. Take a gander at each thing on your ongoing P&L to perceive how it very well may be influenced. Costs will go up - - you need to guess where and how. Once more, incorporate a cost bookkeeping sheet that separates costs expected to meet your deals conjecture. Attempt to consider everything. You'll have to do a hard reasoning and examination to think of legitimate quotes, however doing so will improve your arrangement.

Information

As a general rule, establishing long term financial stability requires profound information about exchange and monetary standards, guidelines, practices and techniques, which could be gained from a progression of learning exercises that exist, and have been set up to create financial momentum. The inquiry could emerge: For what reason is information that significant in creating financial wellbeing? The response to this question begins with the information that assists with tackling issues. During the time spent growing a substantial financial foundation, manufacturers would experience multitudinous issues. Information assists with situating abundance manufacturers in great stead to beat issues as they emerge. The issues of life are by and large better tackled with information. Information levels up abilities. Abundance manufacturers who have obtained information would have their abilities better honed. Information helps basic investigation and laying out the reasoning for taking care of the issues related with growing a substantial financial foundation. Growing a strong financial foundation is a gutsy activity. It is bold as in misfortunes might happen, and those misfortunes can prompt the deficiency of lives and can obliterate families and foundations. Consequently, abundance developers ought to have fabricated their insight base to such an extent that their capacities to go up against issues would be great. A solid information base assists people with taking care of issues without any problem.

Free vs cheap

The expression "free is costly" is much of the time used to imply that something that has all the earmarks of being free or without cost may really have stowed away expenses or adverse results. For instance, a "free" preliminary of an item might expect you to give Visa data, and in the event that you don't drop before the preliminary closures, you will be charged. Or on the other hand a "free" administration might expect you to give individual data, which could be utilized for designated promoting or offered to outsiders. I
Then again, "free" can likewise be thought of as modest, as it requires no monetary speculation and it very well may be a decent worth. In any case, it's essential to consider the expenses and

disadvantages related with something free. It's likewise critical to know about the agreements related with something free and ensure that setting you back more over the long haul is not going.

As a general rule, the expression "free is costly" is utilized to communicate the possibility that something that has all the earmarks of being free may not be essentially as important or gainful as it appears, and that it might include some significant pitfalls

Separate your uses into necessities and needs. Food, asylum, and dress are clear requirements. Add medical coverage expenses to that rundown, alongside collision protection assuming you own a vehicle and life coverage assuming that others are reliant upon your pay. Numerous different uses will only be needs.

Chapter 4
Money vs time

Once spent, time is irreversible, yet cash might be procured back. The rich and the unfortunate actually have a similar measure of opportunity in their day, however the rich approach cash that the poor don't. Cash might be saved close by for some time, however time can't be put away. Time is ceaselessly limited and unabated, while cash might be raised by working harder. Time isn't steady and continues to push ahead, despite the fact that cash might remain something similar for some time. While cash's worth might lessen with time, that of time doesn't.

What is valid riches

Abundance is a mind boggling idea that can mean various things to various individuals. For some purposes, it could bc thc collection of material belongings, while for others it very well might be more about having a feeling of monetary security or opportunity. At last, what is abundance is an individual choice that every individual should make for themselves. Nonetheless, a few normal subjects that rise out of examination on the point include:
Abundance is something other than cash. While monetary security is a significant piece of riches, not by any means the only component adds to an individual's feeling of prosperity. Other significant elements incorporate connections, wellbeing, and individual satisfaction.

Abundance is an excursion, not a destination.True abundance isn't something that you accomplish for the last time. It is a continuous course of development and advancement. As you learn and develop, your meaning of abundance will probably change and advance.

Abundance isn't tied in with having more, yet about being more. Genuine abundance isn't tied in with gathering material belongings. About carrying on with a life is significant and satisfying. It is tied in with being satisfied with what you have and taking advantage of your time and assets.

What is true wealth

Wealth is a complex concept that can mean different things to different people. For some, it may be the accumulation of material possessions, while for others it may be more about having a sense of financial security or freedom. Ultimately, what constitutes wealth is a personal decision that each individual must make for themselves. However, some common themes that emerge from research on the topic include:

Wealth is more than just money. While financial security is an important part of wealth, it is not the only factor that contributes to a person's sense of well-being. Other important factors include relationships, hcalth, and personal fulfillment.

Wealth is a journey, not a destination.True wealth is not something that you achieve once and for all. It is an ongoing process of growth and development. As you learn and grow, your definition of wealth will likely change and evolve.

Wealth is not about having more, but about being more. True wealth is not about accumulating material possessions. It is about living a life that is meaningful and fulfilling. It is about being content with what you have and making the most of your time and resources.

The large accounts

You can't manage what you don't measure. You need to monitor and measure the results of your account management efforts, both in terms of quantity and quality. You can use data and feedback to track and evaluate how well you are meeting your customers' needs, generating revenue, and achieving your goals. You can also use data and feedback to identify and address any issues, gaps, or opportunities in your account management strategy. For example, you can use customer satisfaction surveys, retention rates, upsell and cross-sell rates, or referrals to measure the quality of your account management. You can also use sales reports, dashboards, or analytics to measure the quantity of your account management.

Account management is not a one-time or static activity. It is a dynamic and ongoing process that requires constant review and improvement. You need to regularly assess and update your account management process to ensure that it is aligned with your customers' needs, your team's capabilities, and your business goals. You can use best practices, benchmarks, or feedback to compare and improve your account management process. For example, you can use the Pareto principle, which states that 80% of your results come from 20% of your efforts, to optimize your account management process. You can also use the PDCA cycle, which stands for Plan, Do, Check, and Act, to continuously improve your account management process.

Conclusion

Creating long-term wealth requires patience, discipline, and a well-defined plan. By setting clear financial goals, developing a comprehensive financial plan, adopting a long-term investment mindset, continuous learning, cultivating disciplined saving and spending habits, leveraging technology, and diversifying income streams, individuals can build a solid foundation for sustainable financial success. Remember, the key lies in consistent action, adaptability, and a focus on the long-term horizon.